INTO THIS HOLY ESTATE

INTO THIS HOLY ESTATE
A Story of Staying

Resource Publications
An Imprint of Wipf and Stock Publishers
199 W. 8th Ave., Suite 3
Eugene, OR 97401

www.wipfandstock.com

ISBN 13: 978-1-61097-423-3

Manufactured in the U.S.A.   04/28/2015

for Sheila and Xavier

for Sarah and Chip

and for Tom

fellow long haulers all

Contents

Bless these thy servants
    (pronounces the officiant, this is
    after the exchange of rings;
    he's wrapping you up,
    the hall's booked for lunch)
and sow the seed of eternal life
in their hearts.

And the little seed claps on, like some
    ectopic pregnancy
    in the fallopian tube or the left ventricle
or some more mysterious interstice,
    claps on

to the wall of your marriage,
its inner lining, your *doublure*.

Little 'Eternal' starts to grow, there
    in his secret place,
vegetable to your *potager*, home-grown
if ever there was such a thing.
    Your get.

That whatsoever. . . they shall profitably learn,
they may in deed fulfil the same.

And on and on grows the little seed
    the officiant
spoke and invoked.

The boat's passing has
made music against the shore,

the same that Homer heard.

There goes the wash of the
boat wake
sheushing on the stones

our 'sand-eggs'—as if pebbles
hatch out sand (and they do)

—grains riding up grains
sheushing with each shift

of the mark of the tide
on our little cradle of beach

with its rockers of stone,
rough granite
from elsewhere we

shifted to this shore.
We too shifted to this shore.

And are sifted with time.
That is

time here will sift us of our
less than fine

till we are nothing but pure
passable

stonemeal
fit for a king-
dom.

We used to polish silver.
It was a loving gesture.
I should like to live with that kind of gesture,
that kind of love, that kind of Slow Work.

The monograms say everything.
Though in this province you don't
change the last initial.
Nor did I ever have that kind of silver.

But I have the Slow Work.
And that's enough.
It will have to be enough.

MAS : a name for

where someone has sojourned, where *mansus*—
   the walls of your having dwelt
confessing your dwelling; cognate with *maison*

   so, in the *provençal* psyche, *Mas* :
the name of a place to live
   with walls, with earth to grow things in

to produce produce. And to get, accumulate. So
   sieved by time and continental shift
ours. Here. They speak of the deposit of faith. Yes.

   The deposit of life.
What you have loved, the walls of your
   having loved it

confessing your loving,
   what rests, what resists folly, betrayal, apostasy,
the frailty of our grasp

hobbled as it is in its sling of outrageous
   fortune :
         all you own.
All you mean by home.

I sit on the edge
 of the rocks on the side
 of the beach on the edge
 of the *fleuve*,
my begging bowl in my hand.

Actually, it's a small shallow bowl
for collecting the new beans
 of the second planting
 on the north side
 of the new part
 of the *Mas*,
where it fills, instead, with blackberries

 from the other side of the *pont* we put in
 to cross the creek
 to the *boisé*
and then discovered fiddleheads and *mûres sauvages*.

We also discovered much poison ivy.
Everything is a metaphor.

The begging bowl is for real. I need
whatever sustenance the *fleuve*
can give me.
Beggars are not choosers.

So it fills with wild blackberries
and I think of the helicopter the Evangelical
refused to take
   from off his roof awash
   in the floodpath
   of a hurricane.

No. He trusted too much in God
   to save him
to be seduced
by a mere human and humane response
   to this mortal threat.

In heaven, the drowned man accused God.
You were late!
You promised to send me salvation.
I did, said God. (You know the story.

 God had sent various vehicles,
   finally the helicopter.)
Duh!

And I look at the wild blackberries.
Duh.
And yet,
and yet I return to sit by the *fleuve*.

Begging.
It's a good living, really.
I like helicopters too. (I can give you evidence.)

But there is something
   about an empty begging bowl
which captures what it is about here :

part of the holy estate is
begging with this
emptiness.

We were spared the tin cans tied to the back of our car.
It was a truck anyway.
We were the last to leave the college chapel
salvaging the fanfares of flowers of many May gardens

in our change-to shorts and Tshirts (white)
for loading the marriage mattress onto the pickup
and merriling home where home was then,
many homes ago.

Or not so many, when you think of it. In memory's lint trap
the old farm we rented, then the new we bought,
the village laundry in the Vaucluse turned residence
and let to us,

the digs in the parish hall of one church,
then the *presbytère* of another. Now this.
Home for good.
The *Mas du Refuge* : our 'sweet especial' *mise en scène.*

I never knew that waves
curved to the shape of the shore
but look,

there they come. They do.
The shore

must send out little signals
like radio waves to the water waving in.

'*This* is my embrace! Here. Like this.
Come.'

Or it sends out an imprint, a texture
onto the space

that's between them—dedicated space!—a mould
forming their coming together.

That would be good for marriage manuals.
That would be good for tailors' manuals

for the misshapen,
the much-married.

The water curves in

fitting the curve
the rocks and infant sands

have put to the shoreline,
have put it there with time and tide—

all that's needed
to make a shore.

Getting your shore legs
is marriage seen from the bottom up,
like the doormat for sale on the internet
that reads, 'Hmm! Nice underwear!'
(clutch of skirt to squeezed knees).

There's a lot about marriage
that's from the bottom up.
Of course.
But another thing with shore legs
is that they accustom you
to stability.

The boat doesn't rock any more;
it's beached and blocked.
You see it coming?
Yes : one of the things we say about marriage
(say, in fact, at the point when
the holy wed are locked)
is that this is forever.

Well, not quite forever :
till death us do part.
Till then, we engage to
pledge to these fleshly walls,
this malebody or *this* femalebody
    and not some other.
We commit to shore legs.

And then risk breaking them like thugs.

We are protected by a kingfisher.

He does the rounds of our lot these days
like the Great Pyrenees we had at the farm,
patrolling the boundaries that have fair fallen to us
    from tree to tree to boundary tree
        marked out now
by this small, fearsome, energetic, top-heavy bird
with his pneumatic drill of a voice
    tttttttttttttrrrrrrrrrtt!
Guard Bird with a bark.

He does boundaries like a Pyr.
He does straight lines like a heron.
He hovers like a hummingbird.
He fishes like an eagle.
The wind serves him
but there is no wind today, just that

angelic standing on air :
    his wings
batting sideways in nanoseconds back-forth-back—
    his cravat-tied neck crook'd to see
what might swim in the estuary
of the creek this low tide.
Again and again, sprinkled through his lot-patrols
he hover-bats to check on his luckable provender.

I am allured by the choices birds make :
—why the gull who chose to, chose to
    drop down into the clubhouse meeting on our rocks
while his fellow traveller kept on

—why the particular snowgoose that plummeted,
    plummeted
sideways out of the Easter Dance of the Whole
in that brief, breath-snatching breach of forward decorum,
wingtip leading in free fall
then realigning to join the horizontal company of all.

    A courtship,
because always a second mimicked the first
and the pair rejoined the Whole as a pair

—why this kingfisher has chosen
to make our lot his own.
Courtship.

> *The lines are fallen unto me in pleasant places :*
> *yea, I have a goodly heritage.*

Some sort of incarnation, I'd venture,
some fisher of men.

A rivetter of gratitude.

I cannot sing today.
I am unstrung today, unsung
unheroine making her peace with silence.

Good for you, Emily Dickinson
scribbling away on some roll-top desk
and drawing down the lid

Good for you, Blake, peaceable
in the land of unlikeness

Blessèd are you, Traherne, sole *Centuries* surfacing
in a second-hand bookstore

Good on ya, Merton in double-speak :
naming the cheat of work (you too!) that tries
to build you an identity to outwit annihilation,
    arm against your nothingness

En marche! invincible singers of invisible songs
flailing a way to the infirm,
    snailing away,
blazes of bent wills marking the way :

'Cast a cold eye On life, on death. Horseman, pass by!'

People who read *Moby-Dick*
are tempted to skip chapter XXXII,
the cetology chapter.
They are advised not to.

'Why on earth' (or sea or sky), they say,
'would I want to know this much about *whales*?'
Ah. Because mysteries lurk in those deeps.
Dearly beloved, here beginneth my cytology chapter.

It will be brief. It is already a dispersed chapter.
You will not have more of these sacred words
than you can chew in one mouthful.
Think of it as a diaspora of the married, in words.

Dearly beloved (so it begins)
we are gathered here. . . to join together
this man and this woman in Holy Matrimony;
which is an honourable estate. . . .

There. That wasn't too difficult now, was it.
You watched Kate and William listen to it.
The world watched them listen to it.
No doubt *whales* heard them listen to it.

I just want that citation to remind you of what is
at the base of our meditation, where lie
the deep waters of this honourable estate
whose everydayness so often occludes our vision.

Your estate is not, not merely,
the legacy of your death.
Those parental estates, we all deal with them,
they trip off the tongue, among executors, beneficiaries.

So also do the Darcy Estate, the Wood Estate, acres
of leisure walks and admiration. Upstairs downstairs.
How the other half.
Those are not the deeps we sound.

Estate. Estate.
Roll it round on the tongue
like an old claret. Let it linger, hmmm.
An honourable estate.

When did you last think of yourself
as honourable,
   as in a condition of
honourableness?

When last
   was your way of double being in this world
so true?

What did you promise?
Did you promise?
What wondrous sacred words
   did you disperse upon the holy deeps
for whales to wonder at?

How better or worse are you now,
how richer, how poorer?

My husband
is doing happiness by the shore.

There are so many tasks
he might be doing : bills to be paid,
garbage to be consolidated and put out in the bins,
grass to be cut, fridges to be cleaned before his wife
the gardener and cook arrives with her produce,
    but my husband
is doing happiness by the shore.

By the shoreload he shovels it up,
lying on his birthday *chaise-longue*, a simple investment
worth its weight in incommensurables.
    My husband
measures out his happiness by the *longue*.

No good thinking this is slack time
or that with which he might have furthered the cause,
this *is* the Cause. My husband
is doing it.

No good chafing at his mostly immobility
for the first few waking hours
    while you stir,
stir and shift, run and stoop and reach,
that's not his way; my husband
delves happiness while you spin.

You, of course, spin happiness while he delves.
What is delve for the gander is spin for the goose.
To each his own, the doing of it.
   My husband
does happiness lying by the shore hour by multiple-
hour before his working day begins :
immaterial hours of shovelling by the shore.

If you look closely you can see
just how much of it is down there
   palpably impalpable
crowding the beach like anything, like the autumn's ducks,
like anything really, very much like.

You can see it with your seventh sense.
The seventh sense
is the happiness gauge.
It is like a global positioning system, very much like.
Usually we are too noisy to consult it.
But there it is, its needle flickering
like a diviner divining the source.

If you look closely you can see
   near the source
dictated to you by your global seventh sense
   happiness
a cobalt salt lick
   deliquescing
   into Joy.

So much is done so wrong
    in his name
(it's an old argument) that one
entertains the thought of
disaffiliating, taking off the collar, the easy yoke,
the tacked-on moniker, the habits of collection
    and recollection.
    Not disappearance :
        disapparentness.
I think I will study the fog.

Bonhoeffer from a prison cell
with similar thoughts.
Not same, similar.
Cells wonderfully focus.
Fog wonderfully dissipates.

Let us imagine ourselves a hermit
living in a cell surrounded by fog
and dedicated to the life.
What is one ordained to?
Have we misplaced our epithets?
I would stake my life on this shore,
this manner of meeting of land with water and air.

What I see of the other stuff I begin to doubt
as much as that fellow in the fatal cell.
Disapparentness.

If all goes well we will simply, you and I,
   melt away
becoming fainter and fainter

like the Cheshire Cat's leafy smile
   into the fog
as it steals across the *fleuve*,

we will sit so long on this blessèd shore
   we will forget
how ever we got here

or how (should such a thing
   unimaginably
suggest itself) to walk away

from it, which forgetting
   will not be a bad thing, far
from it!

   —as one might say *near*
from it
as you disapparentize into the foreground
   as it were—

near from it,
proche de vous :
the 'ngd'm has come near from you.

And I have found this refuge like a pearl,
    mine own and not mine own.

For all the years of listening to Shakespeare
    over the Tannoy system at Stratford, thanks,

for all those iambics beating in the ear, the blood,
    the inner ear, the temple, the gut, rendered tragic or comic
by some noble or ignoble voice still recognizably
    Shakespeare, still recognizably,
for all our efforts to exalt it or reduce it, great,
    thanks,

reaching everywhere, the loo, the stairwell, the
    corridor, the dressing-room, another dressing-room,
the props room, the cutting room, yet as camouflaged
    as Birnam forest in the Green Room
where Chris Plummer's darts flew, thanks,

for all that listening for your cue, for all that hearing of it,
    for all that making of entrances and saying those blessèd
lines (whatever he was he was blessed, that is a given,
    some have greatness), for all that mother's-milk so to speak
and for the other kind, it was more scotch than gin, thanks,

for learning that a single malt should not be
    contaminated with ice, should not be so demeaned as to
so to speak act Rattigan instead of Shakespeare, thanks,

for having endured the common fly
  resting on the face of my sleeping Titania, there where
even spraying with toxic chemicals did not quite
  liquidate the problem, try herding flies; fairies, away!
we shall chide downright if I longer stay, thanks,

and for waking to her stranger love;

for Hermia's anger which suited me well,
  for her athleticism which I chose, vixen swinging—
literally—between two suitors turned turncoats,
  and for the blessed final moments of that midnight flight
as dawn breaks on the lovers and Helena finds
  her Demetrius like a jewel, her own and not her own
and I defy that director to ordain again
  that tears and smiles shall not coexist.

And for waking to love in every part,

  thanks. For the phone call that offered me
the part I'd have given my eyeteeth for but had
  undertaken another commitment and didn't see breaking it,
for that turn of events, for every turning point of fortune,
  for the *acedia* that found its way to me, *felix culpa*,
that led to that led to that led to that led to (tracing
  with your finger the golden thread that threads the jewel)
all of it given none of it quite owned, but finally : received.
  With all my worldly goods endowed. This state

the sweet especial scene : tomorrow's bread today.
  And I have found this refuge
like a pearl, mine own and not mine own.

This is the edge of heaven
your feet have hit the grass tarmac cut-bladed as diamond,
 Lewis's arrival station,
you've been bussed to this shore
 this evermore
it is exactly what you most wanted at your best
Each person has what he most loved best :
picking wild blackberries, say, or
sitting on the sand dumbfounded—that's of course me you
 see there
(voice-over of inaudible mouth-music)
(but there is rock and heavy metal elsewhere)

Each thought is caught
the second you think it, in heaven,
no one fumbles the ball,
no barbs adhere to subtexts
there are no texts, the sun illuminates
 a great clarity of understanding,
you have shed
your impatience with your skin,
the intermittent rain washes the stones, your hair
or what takes the place of hair,
 the thunder
claps in Old Testament imitation and it is
God passing indeed, and winking at you
over his literary quote

The bolt that strikes you harms you not a whit
you are out of harm's way; there is no harm
What you thought was harm
is somebody else's loves-best, somewhere in
    another mansion
You would call it hell, but there is no hell
    From here
there is no hell
From there, who knows?

    From here
the changes of the riverface will
present themselves to you forever
you will love them
    forever
you will continue dumbfounded
    never
getting over the astonishment that you are
here and have been
    all along

The rain is firm
at full, long-
enduring, swollen

turgid
as the tools of men
and as fully filling

it comes and comes, this is
sex in the garden

the green receiving
receiving receiving the hammering
all-gentle rain

the lord visiting his
psyche
with the lights out.

One could almost know
on such a day
almost know that

there is marriage
between heaven and earth
and that there is no end to it

Acquiring   Or the knack of the three-
the sitting trot   leggèd race how
letting down into it   when it works you mirror
like so, no longer resisting   your partner, you image
the jouncing around   each other swinging into
 finding the going just fine   that wonderland and
  a fine way of going   you could run
   relaxing your butt   that way
    into it, your spine.   all day
      Letting the partner's body
         embody you in ways
            your body'd
               not've.

What if, thinks my husband, thinking
is a late development
of the evolving species, like
reading silently (taking
the astonished place of
reading aloud), what if

you'd had to discover that you could
have thoughts you hadn't
heard somewhere,
from your own voice, say,
or another's, or another's—
   the old joke : how do I know what I think
   till I hear what I say? but going one better—

what if ratiocination, lovely stuff,
is what we turn to when
our minds are no longer at ease in god
no longer perched at rest
on the edge of our kennels, our paws
hanging over the edge,
   not hungry,
   not tired,
   not fenced but free, what if

contemplation, the art so hard to teach,
is nothing but the animal state
we evolved from

when we were still a peaceable sort
within the evolutionary story, still a cooperative
creature, still part of the kingdom?

What if resting in all this
   recklessly
   heedless of thought
is the reality check *par excellence*?

'Into the whiche
holy estate these two
persones present come nowe to be joyned'
as said the first ever Book
of Common Prayer.

That elegance
of the (redundant) 'the', the
deliberative pace, the Law and the Church
performing their estately minuet
for our *pas de deux*.

Into the which.
Into the said or *ledit saint état*.
Into the unsaid, what didn't make it
into the 1549 Book, or else
what unsaid did :

our common life
otherbody held in common
with onebody one double, as in dealing as in
vision, as in *doppelgänger* as in
till death us do in.

The said Book of
common marriage, with
prayer. The aforementioned
commonplace book
its prayers,

its common stakes
our common mistakes
our uncommon constancy with
said prayer, sung, silent.
The uncommon

book of worthy estates,
the said stakeholders, the worthies,
the which unsaid uponstood common ground
the anonmentioned soil, the
common toil,

the estate-keeper,
the game-keeper keeping statutory score
of/for the aforementioned
dollar worthies.

Ledit projet, the
marriage project, the undertaking of
the said undertaking by the undertakers, partners
in the which project, into the said
and the unsaid

'till death us departe'

the which
holy estate of 'mutuall
societie thone oughte to have of thother'
began as a project
as far back as

paradise :
Eden as was. The Groundworthy.
The which holy common state we penny groundlings
attempt to recapitulate, 'as [it was] once
instituted of God'.

Says the said book.
As did make it into the 1549.
The holy estate into the whiche these two one side the
double 'whiche' : the whom—whom we love,
whom we undertake to love—th'other
holy whiche : the where.

This holy estate
is a *ménage à trois.*
One of them's in bed,
one is down on the shore standing looking
   for the third
—where the fog hides the far
       and middle distance
       and all that shows is
       the near reed growth gone gold with care
       wet in the out and outwards
  of an undemonstrative tide.

He is there.
She knows he is there.
She suspects he is there.

Living with such love
is taxing :
potatoes rest half peeled in the sink
or laundry half dried and left, pages half written
       while the scent of a passing
       is tracked to its den in hopes
of the denizen.

Why should it be
  that the fog,
which hides, the more reveals?
  that the *fleuve*
which they know to be holy should be, should seem, the holier
for the not seeing of?

She sees
the one in bed, and knows that there is holiness there.
Very occasionally her own joy strikes as holy
        at least someone,
        at least herself,
        at least him.

Living with such love as
each of them must experience (is it experience? which them?)
  for the other
  or the others
looks something like the filet beans whose lanky stems
tangle as they
        searching for upwards find sideways
        or even downwards
        and it doesn't seem to
  matter to the crop.

It is occasionally *huis clos chez Sartre*
as she seeks him while he
seeks the him who seeks her and she, still,
stands on the shore, seeking. . . . Yes, sometimes
  it is like that.

Or a cobweb strung between corncob and cob
catches the fog
and sends her scurrying like a spider
  to the still point
to wait, there, at the centre of such wonder-mongering weave.

While he, he is gifted with
a simple, simply intricate method of meeting up with him you
  couldn't call at all analytic, at all,

but it's surely not
the hour-glass waist of that looped
   Victorian lace skirt
   cobweb.

And he tries to serve up chores done and smiles and sweets
   and books to take her mind off.
Ravishment of mind might work—no doubt
how the fog works, so why not.

The motion moves both clockwise and anti-clockwise
   in the *ménage à trois,*
the move
        of holy love, the current.
With a simple switch
you can send the mythic horses prancing motionless
   this way round
   or that.
And who doesn't love a ride on
   such a creature,
   such creatures
   as this, as these, on offer?

They stay at it,
        knowing as well as you can know anything at all
that within this *huis clos* or nowhere
   is the holiness
        that blesses them, that will bless them,
        that once blessed them,
        that can bless them, that is blessing them,
        that will bless them.

The inalienable alterity of the loved one.
I can stand
in the doorway to the kitchen which is large
and watch him
rise from his chair at the table (he looks briefly
up and slightly right as if
hearkening
to a presence, then forgets, or it seems forgets
the presence
or the sensation of a presence, an other, in the kitchen
which is large)

(or perhaps forgetting the forgetting, or even
dismissing
the noticing as if such telltale noticing were not reliable,
were alien
a sense rather of nonsense, or at least alienable, as if living
with such a
permanent sense of another's presence were not the obscure
base or drone
of the unacknowledged music made between his shore
and mine)

and go to
the counter which faces southward to the inalienable *fleuve*
and the toaster
which he puts to use by dropping in slices of bread taken
from a loaf
whose prescience (I speak of the loaf) is moreover
of our being,
his and mine, within this very kitchen where the loaf

is an actor
in the frame in much the same way that we are actors,
bread being
a past master at simulating human being or beingness or
as you might call it
Isness, or Amness, or the thing which is in between
is and am.

And there are those moments when he leaves the house
that I feel both
freed and abandoned, as if those or any eyes like mine looking
now no more
look at me the way I look at him and there is prescience
that that is
how it will be yet I know this is not so, not quite, because
there is
bread on the counter, on the very counter before the very *fleuve*.

The woman taken in anger.
Do you know that pericope? It's missing,
    of course,
but the Holy One writes it on the ground
with his finger, writes it on the heart and writes it
in the sand on the beach :
Thou shalt have no truck with wrath.
Then he lets you go. They all do
    but he's what counts.

From then on you burn with shame
    that ever
in this fair fragile fall of land you found it in you
    to be angry.
You stoke the shame, it is the fairest flame
that ever cauterized your heart,
    you want
never to be without that shame again,
shame for the deed of anger as he

    looks on you
so loving, so generous, so quiet, so clever, so pensive
    he is a whole landscape,
if you could just keep this shame alight
    you might
see him again one day. But that's missing,
too, that eventual bit
    of holy writ.
So you will just have to keep your fingers crossed.

I have now lived almost as much of my life
   with him
as I had lived without before until,
and there is no knowing how this will end.

The wind tugs at the potted strawberry plant on the deck
whose everbearing programme
waits to hit the ground running
   and it is true
that strawberries are survivors, they push
    their way to success.

The strawberry patch is doing very nicely *merci* but
one corner could welcome this stranger.
Some days I am at my
   hope's end.
There is no knowing how this will end, and

some days I doubt my doubts and think we cannot, surely,
not be true to all that we have waded through
   as two as one—
nothing grandiose but life in all its height.

It towers over us like a guardian tree, how can we gainsay
   all those branches?
   —down here
strawberries are survivors; they push their way *merci*
but there is no knowing how this will end.

I thought we were safe
        —as children think they are safe—
in our double being, locked in love like a gear, knowing
just enough of how it worked to drive it, enough of how it
flourished green-thumbed to grow it,
        we were
proper potters, our hearts thrown on the centre.

Here by the windfall *fleuve* everything is up for grabs.
        I won't say
overbearing, but sometimes I feel at my hope's end and
there is no knowing if this end
        is true.

We could do with a stranger *merci*.

There was once a bridge.
It was a small bridge
   over a small river
     in a small town.
It was not a bridge of sighs
   it was a bridge of smiles.

And there was a floating white what
were those things
   we used to wear? Kaftans.
A white kaftan, like a wedding robe
and a mutual avowal of love
and more than that :

a declaration of an inability on the part of
the white kaftan to imagine that
the white kaftan could ever be angry
   with the dark suit.
'I can't imagine ever being angry with you!'
I can't imagine ever being angry with you.
I can't imagine ever being angry with you.

Can you ever forgive this failure of imagination?
You to whom I speak?

What's needed is a heart bypass,
   O you who hold the strings and never pull.

The one with whom you live you
can trust a pair of
scissors with
near your neck,

the one with whom you live you
do the eyedrops of
every night
night after night,

the one you live with as if
irritation were your prized possession
and you wanted to be sure
to share enough of it,

the one for whom you buy the bacon
because he loves it so
then kvetch
that he will eat all the fat on fried bread
and be rushed to hospital,

the one with whom you live you
can shout at when he doesn't
hear, or won't hear,
or shouldn't,

the one you live with you
can read a book beside, over dinner,
and it not (not always) be a measure of estrangement
but of tenderness, your own, that one,
that's the one I mean.

Loving is meaning.
I mean you.

Own.

'Into which holy estate
    [since 1662]
these two
    persons present
come now to be joined.'

Let me rephrase that :
Into which holy estate
    do these two
come now to be joined?

Four words of ancient text
for forty years of puzzlement
    in the wilderness.
I exaggerate of course.

The loftily branching fan-vault heard us,
the pillars of stone echoed our solemn vows,
    and they were solemn,
grave with joy, and they were vows.
And they are.

Pronounced with benefit of clergy,
    guests, good will and
        the secret listener, the Ancient of Words.

But *do* these two
come *now* to be joined?
    What two?
Into which holy estate?
    The daily bread, the daily mess.

A friend visits, talks to us of the book he is writing.
All community involves giving up something.
Even those in perfect agreement
aren't.

There is something each has given up
   perhaps unbeknownst perhaps even to self
to maintain the stance of an accord.
Communion is always, if not a giving in to, yet a giving into,
   face down in the mess.

Our friend's thesis is
   that *civitas* is that, Church is that, even
   marriage is that.

Oh, I'm married all right.
   Un drôle de mariage!
Old heron
   (who's made this home much longer than I)
officiated.

He was the turkey who lives on the hill.
I played pussycat.
        (The local cats who frequent our cathouse
        under the verandahs smock the garden snow in
        winter with their prints, stitching, stitching smocking,
        readying the linen for little Eternal.)

There wasn't an audible ceremony
   for that scene of wedlock
but the stones have heard and echoed
—their sound is gone out—the vaults
   of living branches concurred in the stranger love :

the marriage of a cat to her alley-
shore and its attendant *potager* with its attendant
   house of many stanchions.

The other husband, the owl, makes his appearances
and disappearances, as owls do.
        A good old owl.
Part of the shoreline to be sure. I attempt
not to walk all over him
   as I walk all over my stranger love.

My arms aren't long enough
   and the rocks a bit sharp against the inner flesh
else would I hug my stranger love,
   face down in the dirt.

   Roll over and make angels in the loam, perhaps?
sweeping my garden arms from sides to crown to sides again,
   the angel's skirt my gumboot heels
rooting sideways a pace and back, snouting the soil.

Yes, I could become a true eccentric.
   (Chorus of 'you have, you have, lady!')
I could become a holy fool.
   (Chorus lets that one pass, stymied by the dissonance.)

My husband has his own madness,
I may be allowed mine;
between us we divide *idiot* and *savant* : Jack Sprat.

Vows.
I must consider whether madness
   is the estate we're banded and bound to by them,
trundled along on our hoops of gold and bound for.

Love *à la folie*.
I must give this some thought.

Love O love O bitter love.
How art thou bitter? Let me count the ways.
Newtown.
        Can I stop counting now?

Columbine. Tibhirine. Absalom O Absalom. Princess Diana.
Closer to home René Lévesque and *le beau risque.*
Farther from home Saint Columba sailing into exile.
L'Acadie and *je me souviens.*
The Flight of the Heron, grade six wasn't it,
    reread and rewept in Edinburgh.
Closer to home the merlin hawk at the foot of the big window.
Closer to home Saint Michael.
Closer to home Ardente, the ceremony at the vet's,
the last rites, our eyes
    strung on each other's threads, the fatal dose.
Closer to home the mulberry tree the rabbits
girdled in winter. I know. That's funny.
Take out the mulberry tree. (We did.)
Be serious, Love O bitter love.

You want me to say the cross? I won't.
You want the dart of longing love?
I want sweet. I want calm. What's needed down here is
love O love O peaceful love.
        Life's holding pattern. Kids in it.
        Aren't you the one
who put peace front and centre, O prince of it?
So we want a piece of it.

I will grant you this,
you are always
there,

the most faithful of partners
the most patient
the most unperturbable

every morning I wake and see you
again 'Hello, my lovely!' I say
looking out the window

(you like frames,
pose wonderfully;
you always were photogenic)

admitting.

Your reproach
if it is a reproach
reads like a blessing.

It is your very constancy
which reproaches me for mine—my
constant twisting and turning I know I know

our souls are restless till they rest in you
you think I'm not trying?

And you go on
with your everlovin' beauty
your everlivin' loveliness out there in every

   puff
of breath teasing a dry leaf to the ground
by a hundred   flirtations :
           and one
  twist   turn
     dance
                drop
        curtsey
    float
whisk   flip
      fall.

The leaf has made it to the ground.
Lucky leaf. It rests.

And it was all you,
constant in your playfulness, your patience,
your long-suffering long love :

each bit of independent life
aimed at *me!*—all today's seven billion of us
  each of us a *me!* Aimed at.
Shotgun love.

Sorry! Love, sorry!
Why can't I get this right?

To have and to hold
from this day forward
for better, for worse
for richer, for poorer
    in sickness and in health

They do not mention
for younger for older
they do not mention
for deafer for blinder for weaker
    nor the diaspora of the married faculties

But is understood
for gentler for quieter
for humbler for funnier
and is well understood
for attention for deficit
    for alertness for accident

And is always
(in text or in subtext—the official rite
nothing if not a time-honouring palimpsest)
    this singular commitment :
'With my body I thee worship'.

There you have it, ladies and gentlemen

in all its singularity. And it is perhaps a shame
that the headiness of this odd claim
    is now usually conspicuous in the not saying

And even if it were not singular but reciprocally
confessed by both malebody and femalebody
yet an overweaning prudery prevails and prevents
   such a claim from being owned

Yet there it is :
the body's place in all its glory
   in all this glory

Nor would I, for one, one whit diminish
the illumination this precious text bestows
upon the joint estate
with its unequivocally reasonable accommodation
      of the animal
we live inside and beside and are

And are prepared to worship
according to these vows
and worship with,
      and worship *with*—

Tracing our sex back (two-finger
walking the labyrinth) to the pilgrimage
      of the lonely sperm
towards the complicated egg the mother
carried to you from her mother's womb

Through all its devices and desires :
the arrow
            and the cloud,
the stone
            and the tree,
the tongue and lip of our lung'd animal
worship.

I'd like to be able to tell you about watermelon,
    how much I loved it.
I'd have to tell you about this hot summer.

    I'd like to be able to tell you I grew one, but
that will have to wait till next year
    'if I'm spared'
as they say. (Does that make you laugh?)

I'd tell you how he bought me a whole one, who never
    touches the stuff
(I don't know how that's possible, I don't know
    how he can resist and live) but he bought one for me—

the first time either of us has dared to buy a whole one.
    And how now
that is what we *do* with your watermelons.
    Your whole hog.

And how I come in from the garden and breakfast
    on slices of wedges of the stuff,
pour it down my throat, that's my breaking fast from having
    worked up a sweat in the garden growing things

that next year
    will include watermelon. I'd tell you about that.
About the garden. About the black
    raspberries you will have known were ready to

fall at the fingers' touch into my begging bowl
   that I didn't know were ripe
and came upon by chance positioning something
   near the Frog Corner and

there they were, by the thousands—Unmasked
   Frog Princes : black ripe raspberries.
I grew them.
   I planted them there forgodssakes.

If I told you about watermelon I would get distracted,
   I can see it coming,
I would start gushing about the whole nine yards
   (you know what I mean, the whole 2½ acres)

so for now I won't tell only gush about watermelon.
   What a brilliant idea!
Did you know its taste? Did you plan its pleasure?
   How would you know—without what you gave us, taste-
      buds,
   in a body
      growing?

Did you collude in his saying
'Have you anything here to eat?' Now *that*
   was a brilliant idea.
I would offer him watermelon, in a bowl, with raspberries.

Would he eat it? Would I be able to tell him about them?
   Will I be able to tell you?
What's your plan,
   do we get to talk? Do I get to tell you

how much I loved this garden?
   this shore?
How much I loved what you made and I grew?
   Do I get to say how sorry I am?

The wreathed-crown we wear,
claims the old Syrian hymnwriter
a couple of millennia ago.

The image we are.
The image of a crowned head that flowers
from branches twisted into a round

that always blossoms, that never not.
That never not sings part-songs
round upon round.

You cannot sing a round without somone
else. That's what marriage is.
Singing the daily round.

Always the different entrance.

The *stephanotis floribunda* worn
by Orthodox brides
to be married in, to be joined in, to be flowered

in-under the budding sign of the crown. We were born
for the sign of the crown.
We are all royals.

When we are not cast as Kate and William
we try to wear a fascinator, perky or outrageous, an eyeful
to be sure. To be sure we sport our crowns.

To be sure to prove we are loved of the branch
('the force that through the green fuse').
All this needless showing!

If marriage could be as quiet as the lawn,
the *potager*! The beets, carrots jostle soundlessly
 into jewel-encrusted majesties,

the autumn's offering : the harvest
'the crown of the year' we wear on our feet.
Peace, weariness! Peace!

There is nothing to prove.
There is nothing to gain.
There is everything already.

Perhaps go into the garden and do a bit of loving.
   Perhaps pull on gumboots against the dew
and visit the tide which should be at about the rock
   steps by now, then walk the *Mas* walk.

It's a kind of exercise for the heart muscle,
   aerobics of the soul.
Not much needed but a pair of eyes
   and a pair of feet.

The rest takes care of itself,
that is to say, it takes care of you
   for you—for *it*, too,
for all I know.

The great just-dead Dansereau of Québec
   kept arranging botanical gardens on the strength
of the cooperation that (he reminds us)
   exists between the kingdoms—

the plant and the animal,
   and not shortchanging
the coinage of the mineral and my most-loved
   liquid *fleuve* :

bedrock with a Prince
   to rock to sleep on.
That complicity of life with life is worth the loving.

The thing that makes you drunk
   we neatly call spirits.
We're loaded with them here : cohabitants.
   Drink your fill.
They'll come with us on the *Mas* walk.

   Let me show you
how we've aimed protection
   at the potato patch with that old board fished
out of the creek where it washed down

from the neighbour's kid's pirate plank
   under the culvert.
He's six months older now and
   prefers a motor bike.

At the highest tide of the year the *fleuve*
   comes right up over this rock wall, do you see,
and sucks the soil away off down to Québec,
   to the Maritimes. We've built a frame around

   and the pirate plank's a lid;
we've made a pocket for catching the soil
   for next year.
You can bring on the tide now!

These are the fruit trees we planted.
That apple, no, that was here—since
   oh, a hundred years perhaps. The best there is.
But I fear it's senile, forgets
   to give as many apples as it used to.

We should sing it the orchard wassail
   perhaps. They say it's still done in some parts.
'For more or lesse fruits they will bring,
   As you do give them Wassailing'.

   That window there's
in the bedroom's Frog Corner, named for this north-opening
   casement that gives onto the spring peeper chorus.
Everywhere I've lived it's
   been to the music of frogs.

Here the creek provides music too. And the *fleuve*.
   Round to the front,
if anything is front or back, here, which I doubt,
   is the cloister.

You could do the *Mas* walk round it
if you'd a mind for prayer laps. Mostly
   I'm too busy
weeding or picking, the place being rife with food

   just as those beds to the south you saw are.
Did you know 'rife' relates to 'river'?
Apt, isn't it?
It's all about abundance, about flood.

Planttide and the spirits
   are the only abundance we care about here.
That's part of the loving,
   part of the heart's aerobics. Come. See

the shade garden—that's all it can be,
in this shadowy spot, the pines, firs and spruce
      of another century towering over it,
almost up against the house.

      Not quite.
Here's the front door,
      if anything can be called front or back here.
In the winter, sometimes you have to shovel a tunnel
      to this door from the car.

The snow slides, do you see,
      off the roof here;
it slides back there too onto the cloister briary;
we'll be watching how those brambles do this winter
      when I don't put up protection.
They may pull a Br'er Rabbit on us and thrive the better.

      Or not.
I guess I'd have to say there's
      more to the loving than just what's 'rife'.

But you have to keep at it, I've found that out.
The heart can get senile too, and forget
      to deliver on what it's about or should be up to.
Do you know the old carol

'Jesus Christ the Apple Tree'?
Sometimes I need to sing that, oh
      twenty times in a day,
sometimes the heart ails enough for that.

Do you remember how it. . .?
'For happiness I long have sought'
    you remember? And 'I missed of all'
and then, 'I'm weary

    with my former toil,
here I will sit and rest awhile;
    under the shadow I will be. . . .'

But enough of that. I do not believe,
    by the way,
that the apple is the fruit of the fall.
    I believe he is the fruit of the presence,

the cooperative he has implanted
    into the very nature of things,
here in the wormy soil.
    It won't be the first time

someone has called the heart
    of love an apple.
Rabbouni, here you are!
At last. Here. For you.

After a silence, the bluejay calls
        autumn. 'Fall!
Fall!' he cries, and sometimes 'Hurry!
        Hurry! Hurry!'

There's that moment in late summer, maybe mid-,
        when you notice
that you have not noticed any birdsong in days,
        weeks. When did that

happen? (you wonder), that silence? and go on pulling weeds.
        The crickets have it
to themselves, these days, along with the zizzers
        that still sizzle

in the odd night's heat, and only the gulls carry on as if
        nothing has changed,
and the heron, who gives his occasional *craaaq*,
        and the cat, who

uncultivated goes into heat these days, calling 'All!
        All! Come-Aawwwl!'
feral from her hidden path through the wild sumacs that hide
        the wild blackberries.

Between silence and desire, what is the choice?
        Is there a choice?
Into your desire flows this silence, into such a silence
        hatches your desire—

what the gull did
who played against the wind, surely it was play!
        —aeolian plaything
alone in the silence the day of the big storm,

        hurrying its wings
only to stay in the one place as the storm gathered,
        cruising on idle
whenever the wind let it, the intent just staying there

        sustained on one spot
coasting on that spot as soon as the wind let it,
        playing that wind
like a fisherman playing a fish for all it

was worth, or like a child dancing alone
        just enjoying just
dancing alone, just for all it was worth
        being there.

        And every silent bird
and every silent gardener and every silent garden
        just enjoys just being here.
Wind as love (in a soft land). And we are in love.

The way the horses left.
The way the gentle man
who took over their care when we
rented the farm took them on.

The way he fell in love
and bought his own farm
and took them with him to care for them
till death them might part, which it did.

The way those horses lived
more than thirty joyful years with us, with him
and how they blessed his decision
to draw to a close their palliative care days

and the vet was called in for the last rites.
Asked our permission, that gentle man, with impeccable
courtesy. Got more than ours, as it turned out.
The way they let him know.

The way he saw them go, as he walked back
from their interment in the pasture they had grazed—
    a double rainbow, one from each
in the sky greeting him and giving him the sign of peace.

The way her eyes teared up,
the daughter, watching on the sly
    'Dad is *awesome*!'
her father's escapade at the ballroom competition,

the way love leaks at the eyes
the way marriage is a sacrament
the way love will flow through a marriage
on its way to its destination.

The way the wife said 'Why?
Why is it do you think people marry, Mr. Devine?'
and answered her own question :
'Because we need a witness to our lives.'

The way the eyes tear up at truth named.
The way we need a witness to our lives.
The way we have one.
The way the eyes tear up at beauty so gratuitous it hurts,

how from the first reach of his hand
    to receive her hand
and enfold it in that arm's-length partnership
the upper back adjusts, the neck, the shoulders
adjust, the arms expand the scope of your ribcage to match

the way you're meant to breathe—
the way you're meant to live
and breathe a different air
within the expanse of this close-partnered dance.

The way you hold my hand.
The way you hold the reins.
The way we haunted dressage events
    to see how horse and rider might perfect the art,
love flowing through on its way.

The way you are for me.
The way you choose to be
my witness even to the last pasture,
the way you give the sign of The Peace.

The way you honour your partner
beyond the stirrups, saddle, glove, gown, tails, white tie.
How there is always a partner
    who awaits
the palm of your hand at the end of your arm :

the way I answer Yes,
the way I second-guess
your every dancing move
in this match made of our double witness

and how each is private eye to the other.
And how Fred Astaire remarried in old age a jockey
half his age who will have known
something herself of this same art or nature.

The way the great stallion Hickstead died in the ring
after completing the 13-fence course,
his great heart bursting giving more than his all to Lamaze
and the nobility that brings tears to the eyes like beauty.

The way you choose to dance.
The way you take the chance.
The way your steps advance
as you strike more beauty with your match than

ever you thought possible in this life
especially in your hand,
especially yours,
where you thought but faint dark guttered.

The way you wear your shoes.
The way they come in twos.
The way you want to dance
before it's too late and the invitation gets lost in the shuffle—

no, no, they can't take that away from you.

All Souls'. So still on the *fleuve* one duck can
draw a wake the length of the St-Lawrence Seaway
   as a jet can leave a pen-line
trail across the infinite sky
a thin white line.

The black duck is swimming
and drawing his white wake against
the marine of the *fleuve*'s reflection of
   the far dark bank,
the one that goes so rose-peach some sunsets.

Now just a backdrop for a purposeful duck.

Closer to, two ducks draw two lines dark
against the white near-shore flow
where the *fleuve* reverts to mirroring white sky,
   white heaven, white nothing—
angels' wings, invisible snow geese perhaps.

All, souls. All at our Slow Work. Imagine.
We share this space.

And leave our trails, thin as lines across its face,
across the face of old God.
We are the wrinkles,
the very thinnest of
the lines in God's
dear old
mother-
face.

The snow from every window
　　　　you see it
snowing down like goose down
　　　　you see it
eiderdowning the sleeping earth
　　　　the sleeping beasts

even the squirrel today
has squirreled himself away

somewhere they delight in long summer
　　　　heat waves and fronds of palms
　　　　don't they
where the weather plays a different set
　　　　of variations
　　　　so I'm told

somewhere they grieve
　　　　for the melting ice caps
haunting the memory of the future
　　　　its methane breath of rot, its homeless polars
　　　　bleak past thought
but here. . .

(the feral cat *en catimini*
　　　　today has picked her way to the makeshift manger—
an old skylight propped
　　　　against the bedroom's outer wall
with a bedding of hay away from the worst
　　　　of the wind—and

had her morning ration; her wildness delights me,
   her canny cadging
off my sentimental streak, her single parenting
   down by the beach
among the rocks, her kittens pouncing on their
   tails, their shadows,
    each other)

but here. . . the snow
   you see it
pull its monk's mantle over the jumble of débris
   we never quite get rid of
under the evergreens outside the window of
   the loo with a view—
one of the loos with one of the views—
   this one the evergreen
boughs yoked with snow, light, burdened
   with light, with white
   you see it

clean the mess of our lives there like so much
   shed sin gets
cloaked in fresh snow's luminous burden the desert
   monk pulls over you
as you slip up yet again or some god
   pulls over you

or someone some monk listens to daily (in the
   interstices of prayer
where someone happens like an event)
   pulls over you

whose wildness delights me.

I get ready to go for the *Mas* walk and
    the *fleuve* goes crazy
with excitement, jumping up and down,
    spinning round and yipping, biting its tail in glee
here we go!-here we go!-here we go!
No leash today, just bust out and crash about
    wild joy, wild waves, wild wildiness—*ouf*!
What it is to take the *fleuve* for a walk.

All day the corn bends over, the trees bend over
    the lightweight chairs bowl over, the leaves
quit the trees there's raking for you! for the future.
    The solid heavyweights just
    take it all in, mmm, fall, yep :
chairs of substance—found in a fine old
    secondhand farm furniture trove back in Ontario.
Picking up French as they can, now.

I get ready to go to bed :
the ritual of the toothbrush, the paste going on,
    the mouth going sudsy, the lip of the glass a bit caked withal,
the ritual of the last pee, the glass of water
    by the bed, getting the pillows right, the sheets fair,
has he got his share, have I,
the ritual of Compline, so quiet in the dark, recited
    from memory, he falls asleep in the middle,
wakes up, carries on, if I ever hear the end it's a bad night
    but mostly I hear through the names we pray for,
others' sisters, daughters, brothers,
    then the special ones and then
some we don't know but wish well in their steep task.

I get ready to go,
  put my house in order,
finish unpacking so they can pack it up again
  when the time comes,
with a clear order and a clear conscience.
I'll label things like my mother (one of the kind
  who kept pieces of string too short to use
and labelled them 'too short to use', yep).

I get ready to go.
  That's okay.
Days like this
  I can even take it in my stride.
There's digging for you, for the future.
  Your turn soon enough.
Ready for another *Mas* walk?

In our kitchen sit three chairs.
One each for us and
          one for the silent partner.

Our hearing's not always
quite as good as it could be
          at catching silence, his many nuances.

But all is not lost on us,
not least the many words for 'snow'
          the 'o' of it
or it may be the 'o' of 'wow'
          or of 'you'
          or of 'love'.

You can walk out as if on a pier
        thrust into winter—
waves of white all round you from last wind's antics
        the sun like a seaside.

And all this cold chills you not a whit
        because
you have just entered the bedroom.
        Entering the bedroom
is walking out onto this pier interior—
        into your goodly heritage
        your gardens asleep at your feet.

Into this holy estate.
The glass all around.
        Occasionally
a wall trumps a window, but mostly
furniture sits on the floor on the carpet as if it were
        kindergarten, as if it were
the junior school assembly.

And from there, you stare up at the Big World.
Everything is interesting to this school assembly.
There is everything to learn.

Why, for instance, you are here at all
        when there are refugee camps in Turkey, Haïti, Sudan.
Why there is heaven at all when there is hell.

You will never answer.
You will never know the answer.
You will never again know much beyond
        these frontiers
of the distant land of achievement.

Is it bleak in winter? they ask.
I guess it's too much in winter, they guess,
        all that. . . (voice trailing off)

                            —what? wildness?
—what? weather?—what? nothing? Too much?
You are falling in love with nothing.
Nothing has been achieved. It is all you have
        of achievement
this barricade :
  'begging with this
  emptiness' :

pop-eyed pleasure of the junior school assembly
at all this Big World out there being, in here being—
the heart-throbbing, sense-coddling, joy-privileging
        never meant to be *fair* gain
this limb interior is

thrust out over the *kindes garten*'s snow
        liminal world of winter at work—
at work at rest.

This is the Land of Likeness.

I'm thinking of writing
a book with a one-word title : *Oh!*
On the cover is 'Oh!'
When you turn to page one
you find 'Oh!'
Turn to page two it's the same thing.
There is only one word in the book;
   it is 'Oh',
   page after page.

The reviews come out and they say, 'Ohhhh!'
   One of them says, 'Oh? *No.*'

I'm already planning the sequel.
It's called, *Look!*
   The reviews aren't out yet.

I confess the mystery of why we are here.
I confess the lack of just deserts, the outrageous fortune.
I confess the lack of deserts. Ice may pack a wallop
but it's water in disguise, not parch of sand.
I confess the water.

I confess the lack of pitched tent roofs lining the parched sand.
I confess the cathedral roof of our sleeping space
above the king-size bed. I confess the bed,
the scandal of the dissonance between
the bleak miles of refuge of the refugees

and this brief Eden of our Refuge.
I confess the radiant warmth, the *air climatisé*,
the hydroelectrification of everything that cooks,
shoves, cleans, heats, splits, joins, pumps, lights, cools,
sounds, plays, texts and connects.

The sanitation, I confess that, the absence of cholera, TB, HIV,
malaria, polio, bullets, snipers, incendiaries,
drones, corpses, rodents. I confess
to the odd monotone drone. The odd mouse.
One in hand worth two in the cookies.

I confess to laughter.
On the edge of the grave I confess to laughter.
Every grave. And to children. Our get, all of them
of all of us. Everywhere.
God willing always.

Dearly belovèd,

We used to polish silver,
milk goats, take planes, any number of things
that may or may not have got us ready
for this.

How little is basic!
The rights campaigners have it wrong :
it is so very little we have actually
a *right* to.

There is a sound I hear in my head,
it is the sound of two feet—
andante.
It is like one hand clapping,

an empty
theatre, a runthrough of one and
the director watching, the type who gives
notes after the last performance.

The rustle of leaves, scuffling
of shoes or boots, just two, not four though
four was nice; agreeable, wasn't it? I hear this sound
in my head

maybe you do too. It may be we have a right to *it*.
It goes like this, in a language I'm groping for,
it's like a melody, what they call
a brainworm :

"walking rhythm, something in mind
   ma non troppo,
moving from here to somewhere, say here,

   then the same again. If there is eagerness it is
banked fire.
   Just walking, *andante,* one leg and then the other in time

and its allotted space, the foot and the eye taking
   the minute measure of the day
in a place of some certain earth and growth, some air

   and some tide,
two feet and two eyes
   at their peregrinatory basics with the aid of

legs, of time out of mind *ma non troppo*
   and of a route to take,
to take to the rhythm of walking : like

   the leg over leg of
leggy love-making those early
   days of being an ordinary married couple

newly old- ,
   newly quotidian and we joked it was going
'walking'

   the nightliness of it (is there a word? quotinoctly?)
of that ordinary moving
   the *andante* of your cherished hearth and its banked fire—

the smooring that holds the flame
   ready to burst into another day, another
first footing, another

   first caressing
the earth with the sole of your foot, and again, and again,
   and the little corners of the mouth ready—

not the burn-off of the 400 metre sprint, its dash,
   not your ambitious cardiovascular
nor the half-marathon

   just sentence after sentence of a sort of meaning
without the compression
   on the spine of theological weight-lifting, without the tantric

gymnastics of syntax
   just a sort of meaning to be, a sort of meaning to say
what I mean to say,

   to look : that is to walk and chew gum so to speak;
to walk and look, and say.
   The earliest words in a foreign language."

The MAS is my refuge; I shall not want.
It giveth me to lie low by these moving waters.
It engraveth me the initials of my married name, my estate;
it silvereth me a monogram where was no wedding set.
Yea, though white o'erlay all green that groweth,
and all blue that moveth; yet will I stay
in this Thin Place. For I do
shore up hope; that it
hath been since
for ever.

Medled lyf. One foot before one foot beyond.
   A mixed marriage. In the world but only partly *of* it.
Semi-cloistered. Out of it by halves.
   A middling silent Order.

We are pledged to these walls, the four King's Corners
   of this bed. Each passing novitiate year
makes it clearer we are inching towards
   our solemn professions.

Roads pass, cars, we can hear them, we watch the news,
   read the internet, enter R/Vs in our agendas,
not infrequently shop. But we are retracted from the world
   like snails touched, simpletons, touched

and confirmed in our living 'continually more and more'
   the house and office of the *medled lyf.*

The middled life, mulled wine, toast.

oOo

www.ingramcontent.com/pod-product-compliance
Lightning Source LLC
Chambersburg PA
CBHW071105090426
42737CB00013B/2496